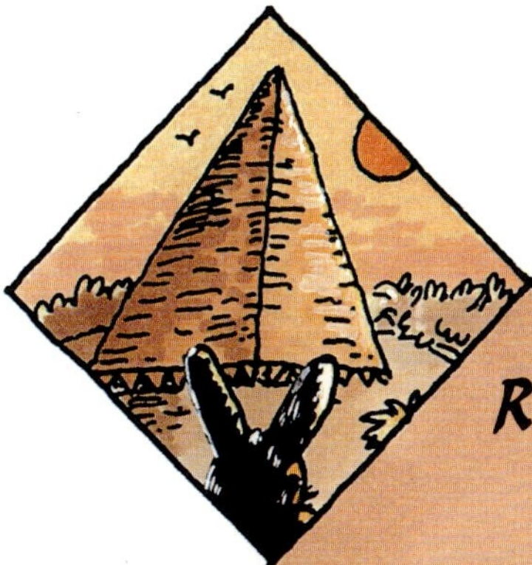

RUDLEY CABOT IN...

# THE CARROTS OF DOOM

Keith Brumpton



Orion
Children's Books

*For their help with this book I'd like to thank Jane and Judith, and also Sarah.*

*For specialist information on Ancient Rabbitology I'm indebted to Professor Omar Ben Ali at Oldham University, and to his colleague, Miss Nefertiti Laithwaite.*

*Rudley Cabot's exploration gear was kindly donated by Rabbit Leisurewear Ltd., of Kidderminster.*

Keith Brumpton.

*Penzance Pier, 5 am, July 29th*



First published in Great Britain in 1995
by Orion Children's Books
a division of the Orion Publishing Group Ltd
Orion House
5 Upper St Martin's Lane
London WC2H 9EA



A catalogue record for this book is available from the British Library
Typeset by Deltatype Ltd, Ellesmere Port, Cheshire
Printed in Great Britain
ISBN 1 85881 078 7 (For HB)
ISBN 1 85881 153 8 (For PB)

# Contents

# THE CARROTS OF DOOM

Many, many years ago, in the time of the Ancient Bungyptians, during the reign of the Great Fur-O Tutenkhabage, a war was waged against the Weasel Kingdom in the south.

The Bungyptians won a great victory and brought home many treasures. To their amazement they also discovered a strange device made of silver carrots, which had the power to turn ordinary objects into gold.

Although this fantastical device brought Tutenkhabage much wealth, it gave little happiness to his kingdom, and it was said that the carrots were cursed.

For this reason, rabbits began to call them "the Carrots of Doom". Eventually, after years of misfortune and failed lettuce crops, the Fur-O decided to get rid of the Carrots of Doom.

He instructed his High Priest, Rab-E-Buns, to hide them in a place where no rabbit would ever find them again. And to this day, no rabbit ever has . . .

## Episode One

# A LOAD OF OLD RABBOGLYPHICS

Rudley Cabot was talking to his friend, Professor Rachel Becker, about her new job at the Museum of Rabbit History.

* **Rabboglyphics**: A form of picture writing developed by Ancient Rabbits

I'M NOT CERTAIN YET, MIND YOU, BUT EACH DAY I LEARN A LITTLE MORE.
look of excitement
IT CERTAINLY SOUNDS LIKE AN ADVENTURE IN THE MAKING.
TODAY I HAD A VISIT FROM AN EXPERT CALLED DR RATSKILL TO SEE IF HE COULD HELP, BUT HE COULDN'T WORK OUT ANY MORE THAN I CAN...
HE WAS VERY HELPFUL THOUGH MY MAIN WORRY NOW IS SECURITY... THERE HAVE BEEN ONE OR TWO INCIDENTS RECENTLY.
DO YOU THINK SOMEONE MAY BE AFTER YOUR SCROLLS?
I'M NOT SURE. BUT IF THEY DO REFER TO TREASURE THEN OF COURSE SOME PEOPLE WOULD BE VERY KEEN TO TAKE A CLOSER LOOK. SO IT'D BE BEST IF YOU KEPT THIS CONVERSATION TO YOURSELF...

rrrrumble
CRACK!
GOODNIGHT, RUDLEY. SEE YOU SOON.
NIGHT. AND GOOD LUCK WITH THE SCROLLS.
♫
mysterious stranger

# Episode Two

# SCROLL CALL

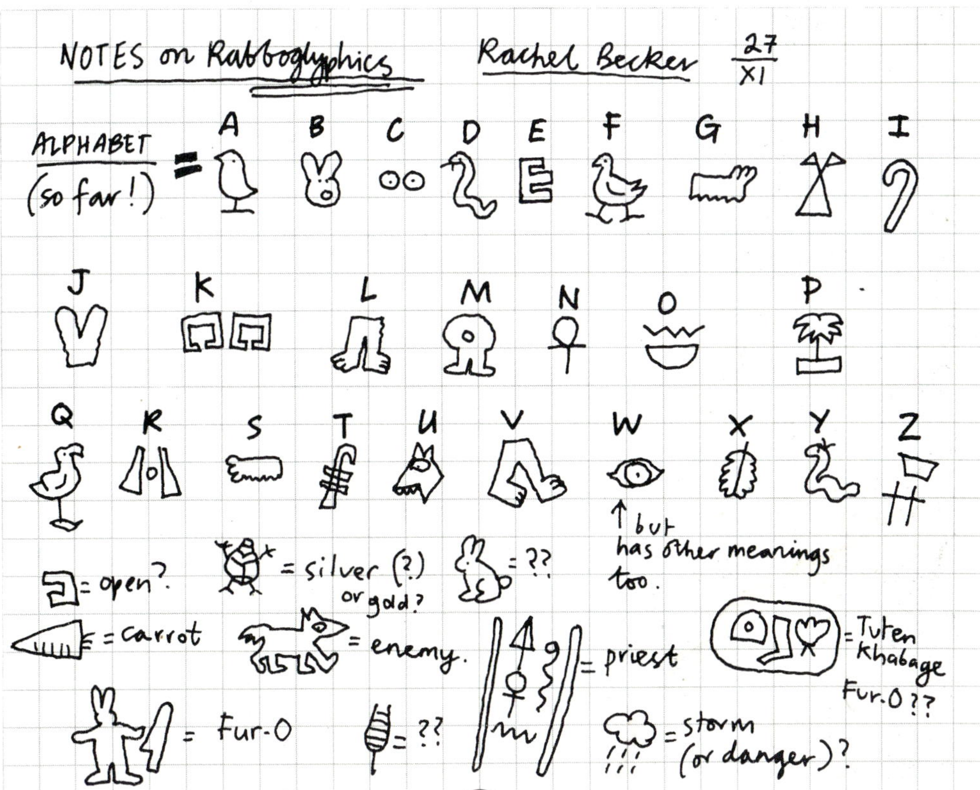

PIECE BY PIECE IT'S COMING TOGETHER...
I DON'T BELIEVE IT! THE LAST SCROLL REFERS TO THE WHEREABOUTS OF THE CARROTS OF DOOM!!!
ADVANCED RABBOGLYPHICS
OMAR B. CARROT
DEADLY TREASURE... WORTH A FORTUNE...
THIS IS HOT STUFF! I'LL HAVE TO TREAD CAREFULLY FROM NOW ON...

Outside a storm rages . . .
The museum is filled with strange shadows . . .
Suddenly the building is plunged into darkness . . .
HEY, WHO TURNED OUT THE LIGHTS?
Rachel hears a door open behind her, and deep, muffled voices . . .
HELLO?
!

WHO ARE YOU? HOW DID YOU GET IN? ALL THE DOORS ARE LOCKED...
THAT'S REALLY NO CONCERN OF YOURS, PROFESSOR.
WHAT DO YOU WANT HERE?
JUST KEEP QUIET AND YOU WON'T GET HURT. NOW HAND OVER THOSE SCROLLS!
ER, BUT WHAT WOULD YOU WANT WITH THEM? THEY'RE JUST A LOAD OF OLD RABBOGLYPHICS...
TIE HER UP, THEN GRAB THE OTHER SCROLLS!
snatch
RIGHT, BOSS.

And with that, the masked intruders vanished into the night, along with the priceless scrolls. Rachel remained a prisoner until morning, when the visiting expert, Dr Burdock J. Ratskill, arrived at the office.
GREAT BUNCHES OF CLOVER, RACHEL, WHAT HAPPENED? ARE YOU ALLRIGHT?
I'M OK, BUT THE SCROLLS HAVE GONE...
THERE WAS A GANG OF THEM... THEY TIED ME UP. I'M SORRY, DOC, THERE WAS NOTHING I COULD DO.
IT LOOKS LIKE YOU'VE HAD A WASTED TRIP.
AS LONG AS YOU'RE SAFE, MY DEAR, THAT'S THE MAIN THING.
I WAS SO CLOSE TO MAKING AN IMPORTANT DISCOVERY. I HAVE TO FIND THOSE SCROLLS AGAIN!
SURELY IT WOULD BE SAFER JUST TO FORGET ALL ABOUT THEM?
IT PROBABLY WOULD, DOCTOR, BUT THAT'S NOT THE WAY I WORK.

## Episode Three

# CABBAGE BAR RENDEZVOUS

Holly's Cabbage Ba
RUDLEY!
RACHEL, HI, HOW ARE YOU? IT'S SOME WEATHER WE'RE HAVING!
CLOSED
Over a cup of hot chicory, Rachel quickly described the events of the previous evening . . .
... SO YOU THINK THAT GANG STOLE THE SCROLLS BECAUSE THEY CONTAIN SOME SORT OF INFO ABOUT THE CARROTS OF DOOM?
THAT'S MY GUESS, THOUGH DOCTOR RATSKILL DOESN'T AGREE. HE THINKS ANOTHER MUSEUM MAY BE BEHIND THE ROBBERY.
MM... THAT DOESN'T STRIKE ME AS VERY LIKELY.
NO.
YOU SAID YOU'D ALREADY WORKED OUT SOME OF THE WRITING?
YEAH... QUITE A BIT.
WERE ANY PLACE NAMES MENTIONED?

THERE IS ONE NAME THAT KEPT CROPPING UP...
BUNZA.
BUNZA!
suspicious-looking character.
BUNZA?!
WHERE'S BUNZA?
IT'S THE SITE OF THE GREAT PYRAMIDS.
...MANY HOPS TO THE NORTH OF COLONY 27X. RUDLEY, I NEED SOMEONE TO HELP ME TRY AND RECOVER THE SCROLLS... AND I THINK THE OBVIOUS PLACE TO START WOULD BE BUNZA.
I KNOW IT'S A LOT TO ASK, BUT BELIEVE ME, THEY COULD BE REALLY IMPORTANT... ESPECIALLY IF THEY ARE LINKED TO THE CARROTS OF DOOM.
AND I WOULDN'T REALLY WANT TO FACE THAT GANG OF HOODED THIEVES ON MY OWN.
THAT'S AS CLEAR AS A STICK OF CELERY ON A MOONLIT NIGHT.

OF COURSE I'LL HELP. IT SOUNDS LIKE WE SHOULD GET OURSELVES TO BUNZA AS FAST AS POSSIBLE. I'LL CALL YOU TONIGHT AND WE CAN MAKE ARRANGEMENTS.
OK, HERE'S MY BURROWPHONE NUMBER...
THIS COULD BE A DANGEROUS BUSINESS, RUDLEY, THANKS FOR HELPING.
TONIGHT
NO PROBLEM. WE'LL BURROW OUR WAY TO THE BOTTOM OF THIS, JUST YOU WAIT AND SEE!
THAT'S WHAT YOU THINK!
THE BUN
MISSING SCROLLS... HOODED INTRUDERS... WHAT A DAY!
I COULD DO WITH A QUICK NIBBLE TO TAKE MY MIND OFF THINGS.
TAKE AWAY TURNIPS
24 hour

## Episode Four

# BACK TO PACK

IN FACT I THINK IT COULD BE VERY DANGEROUS.
The skies over Rabbit Colony 27X were dark and filled with rain as the two rabbits set off for their meeting with Rachel.
Their departure was observed by a figure hidden on the other side of the street . . .
Rachel was waiting to meet them, together with her colleague, Dr Ratskill, who wished them all good luck.
YOU'RE VERY BRAVE TO GO AFTER THE SCROLLS LIKE THIS. IF I WAS A FEW YEARS YOUNGER, I'D COME WITH YOU MYSELF.
BUT PLEASE DON'T TAKE ANY UNNECESSARY RISKS...THIS GANG OF ROBBERS SOUND LIKE A DANGEROUS BUNCH... VERY DANGEROUS.

* **1 mega-hop** = 2 human miles

TAXI
ARE YOU SURE THIS IS THE WAY TO THE HARBOUR?
TAXI
WE'VE BEEN KIDNAPPED!
TAXI
THERE'S A SCREEN BETWEEN US AND THE DRIVER, SO HE CAN DO WHAT HE LIKES!

HA·HA·HA!
VROOM!
I'VE JUST HAD AN IDEA, CAB... PASS ME THOSE ICEBERG LETTUCES FROM YOUR LUNCH·BOX.
??!
NOW HOLD ON TIGHT WHILE I LEAN OUT OF THE WINDOW!
TAXI
TAXI
Fut·Fut

!
THE TAXI IS SLOWING DOWN!
SHOVING THOSE LETTUCES IN THE FUEL TANKS HAS WORKED!
THEY MADE THE ENGINE MISFIRE.
OK, EVERYONE OUT AND LET'S HOP IT!!!
HEY, COME BACK!
TAXI
I THINK WE'D BETTER HEAD FOR THE HARBOUR ON FOOT THIS TIME!
THEY DIDN'T EVEN PAY THEIR FARE!

## Episode Five

# BOUND FOR BUNZA

A land of volcanoes . . .
dense forests of broccoli . . .
great heat . . .
and savage beasts!
WE'RE STILL AT LEAST TWENTY MEGA-HOPS FROM BUNZA!
OH NO! AS MUCH AS THAT!
Water supply
I'D BETTER NIP BACK TO THAT STREAM AND GET SOME MORE WATER.

But though Rachel struggled for all she was worth, she still couldn't escape, and was dragged off into the jungle.

LET'S NOT THROW IN THE LETTUCE YET...
RACHEL IS PRETTY SMART FOR A HUMAN. IF WE CAN FOLLOW THOSE FOXES, THERE'S STILL A CHANCE WE CAN RESCUE HER.
I SMELL FOXES THATAWAY!
twitch
YOU'RE DEAD RIGHT, CAB, LET'S GO!
LOOKS LIKE THEY'RE HEADING FOR THE PYRAMIDS AT BUNZA!
ALL ROADS SEEM TO LEAD TO THE CARROTS OF DOOM!
YOU CAN SAY THAT AGAIN. AND SINCE I'M A PARROT, I PROBABLY WILL.

# Episode Six

# OUT-FOXED

LET'S DIG A BURROW FOR THE NIGHT.
WE'VE GOT A BIG DAY AHEAD OF US AND MY PAWS ARE WEARY.
'Burrow'
TIME TO FINISH THOSE BUNNIES!
REACH FOR THE SKY, RABBITS...
OOOF!
HE FELL INTO THE BURROW!
THERE'S RACHEL!
BUNZAI!
BIFF!

A desperate struggle ensued . . .
KNEW MY FISHING NET WOULD COME IN USEFUL!
LET'S GET OUT OF HERE!
THOSE RABBITS CAN REALLY MIX IT!
Finally Rudley and Cabba were able to scamper over to Rachel and set her free.
GREAT WORK, TEAM. THAT WAS A TIGHT SQUEEZE.
AS THE RABBIT WITH THE SMALL BURROW SAID.
Next day . . .
WE SHOULD SEE THE GREAT PYRAMID AT ANY MOMENT.
HOW CLEVER THOSE ANCIENT BUNGYPTIANS WERE . . .

As far as the eye could see there were fantastical buildings . . .
built long ago and now almost (but not quite) fallen into ruins . . .
LOOK! THE GREAT PYRAMID OF BUNZA!
I WONDER IF IT CONTAINS THE ANSWER TO ALL THESE STRANGE SHENANIGANS?
LET'S HOPE WE MANAGE TO GET THERE IN TIME TO FIND OUT!

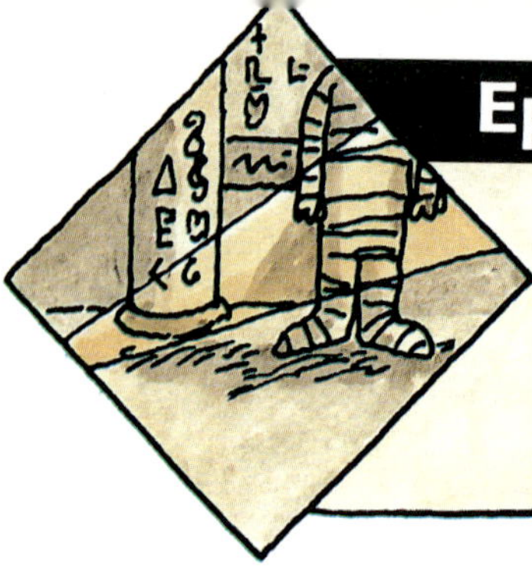


## Episode Seven

# CONCERNING WHAT'S HID...

LOOK AT THIS, RUDLEY. WHAT A VIEW!
NO TIME FOR THAT, CAB... THE TRAIL HAS GONE DEAD. HAVE YOU GOT AND IDEAS, RACHEL?
WELL, IT'S A BIT OF A LONG-SHOT, BUT I'M JUST WONDERING IF THE ANSWER LIES INSIDE THE PYRAMID?!
IF IT DOES THEN WE NEED TO FIND AN ENTRANCE.
HEY!
LET'S TRY THIS WAY... SOME OF THESE BUSHES HAVE BEEN MOVED QUITE RECENTLY.
IT'S CERTAINLY WELL HIDDEN!
COULD THIS BE THE WAY IN?

* use Rachel's notes on page 9 to decipher the Rabboglyphics (in this book)

HANG ON, I THINK I'VE GOT IT ...
EACH LETTER OF THE ALPHABET IS REPLACED BY THE LETTER THAT COMES ONE PLACE BEFORE IT... SO
BECOMES...
PRESS/THE/LEFT/TRUMPET!
Carving of trumpet
IT'S OPENING!
TO REVEAL A SECRET PASSAGE!
OPEN SESAME!
tremble
'STRUTH!
STRIKE A RADISH!
OK, EVERYONE. GRAB A TORCH AND LET'S GO!
IT'S SO DARK...
AND CREEPY!
WHICH WAY?
THAT WAY WILL DO NICELY. HA-HA-HA!

THIS PLACE SMELLS AS MUSTY AS A FOX'S SOCK DRAWER!
YEAH, BUT WHAT FANTASTIC PAINTINGS!
EH?
DON'T WORRY, RUDLEY, IT'S ONLY AN ANCIENT TOMB...
OF COURSE! SO IT CONTAINS THE BODY OF ONE OF THE FUR-O'S ADVISERS OR FAMILY...
IT LOOKS A BIT SPOOKY IF YOU ASK ME.

LOOK AT ALL THAT GOLD! MUST BE WORTH A BOB OR TWO.
Suddenly the ancient tomb began to open with an eerie creak . . .
THAT'S RIGHT, TWITCHY NOSE! IT'S WORTH A SMALL FORTUNE. HA-HA!
shocked look!
DR RATSKILL!
THE THIEF!
I'M AFRAID SO. THOUGH I WOULDN'T BLAME DOCTOR RATSKILL... AFTER ALL, HE DOESN'T REALLY EXIST!
Peel
IT WAS A MASK!
HA-HA-HA-HA-HA.

CAPTAIN WEASEL!
BUT YOU'RE...
LOST IN SPACE? *
discarded disguise
NOT QUITE, MY FLUFFY FAILURES...
I WAS RESCUED BY ANOTHER SHIP PILOTED BY SOME PIRATE FRIENDS OF MINE...
ALLOW ME TO INTRODUCE THE CREW OF THE "GRUBBY FOX."
!
!
!
AND WITH THEIR HELP I NOW HAVE THE SCROLLS THAT WILL LEAD ME TO THE CARROTS OF DOOM!
* See The Quest for the Golden Carrot
HA·HA·HA·HA!
I SHOULD HAVE GUESSED! THAT'S WHAT HE'S AFTER!

## Episode Eight

# MORE TIGHT CORNERS THAN A GERBIL'S CAGE

DON'T PANIC, WE'RE NOT FINISHED YET...
OUR PAWS MAY BE TIED, BUT CAPTAIN WEASEL FORGOT ONE IMPORTANT THING ABOUT RABBITS...
WE'VE GOT GOOD TEETH!
NOW BEND THIS WAY, RACHEL, WHILE I GNAW THROUGH THAT ROPE.
Suspended above the snake pit, Rudley hardly dared look below as he and Cabba chewed their way through the ropes that were holding them.
Meanwhile, the snakes hissed . . .
A subterranean breeze wobbled their platform . . .
But at last . . .
PHEW! I'M THROUGH.
NOW WHAT?
wobble
NOW WE TIE THE PIECES OF ROPE TOGETHER...

MAKING A LOOP AT THE END...
TAKE IT, RACHEL, YOU CAN PROBABLY THROW IT FURTHER THAN WE COULD.
JUST LIKE THE WILD WEST!
GOOD SHOT!!
HERE GOES!
SSSSSS
THAT WAS THE MOST FRIGHTENING BUNNY-JUMP EVER!

REMEMBER... DON'T LOOK DOWN!
WHY NOT?
BECAUSE IT'S TERRIFYING.
DON'T WORRY, CAB, YOU CAN DO IT.
HOLD ON TIGHT!
stakes. ouch!!
Cabba and Rachel kept their nerve, held on tight, and joined Rudley on the other side of the snake pit.
WELL DONE, EVERYBODY, THAT WAS A CLOSE ONE!
CAN I SNEEZE NOW?
TCHOO!

## Episode Nine

# MUMMY'S THE WORD

IT MUST HAVE BEEN HIDDEN THERE FOR CENTURIES!
NOW I'VE HAD A CHANCE TO STUDY IT I CAN HARDLY BELIEVE WHAT WE'VE GOT HERE...
THE LAST SCROLL OF RAB-E-BUNS, THE FUR·O'S HIGH PRIEST, IN WHICH HE DESCRIBES WHERE HE HID THE CARROTS OF DOOM!!!
BRILLIANT! BUT CAN YOU UNDERSTAND IT?
MOST OF IT, YES, BUT IT ENDS WITH A RIDDLE.
IT'S SO QUIET IN HERE... LIKE AN ABANDONED WARREN.
RIGHT, BUT LET'S NOT FALL INTO ANOTHER TRAP... CAPTAIN WEASEL AND HIS PALS ARE BOUND TO BE SOMEWHERE ABOUT.
I DON'T THINK SO. THEY DON'T HAVE RAB-E-BUNS' SCROLL, SO THEY CAN'T KNOW WHERE HE FINALLY HID THE CARROTS OF DOOM. NOT EVEN THE FUR·O HIMSELF KNEW THAT.

SOMEWHERE BEYOND THIS ROOM LIES A SECRET PASSAGEWAY TUNNELLED BY RAB-E-BUNS HIMSELF.
A HIDDEN BURROW!
Suddenly Rudley spins round . . .
WHO'S THERE?
EEK!
I AM THE GUARDIAN OF THE FUR-O'S TOMB . . .
NO BODY MOVE A MUSCLE, AND PREPARE TO MEET YOUR DOOM . . .

TIME FOR A SHARP EXIT!
nail
LOOK!
THAT'S NO MUMMY! IT'S ONE OF CAPTAIN WEASEL'S CREW.
YEAH, BUT THAT STILL ISN'T GOING TO HELP YOU!
THIS OLD CEREMONIAL TRUMPET COULD COME IN USEFUL...
CAN YOU PLAY?

NO...BUT I HIT THE RIGHT NOTE!
CAPTAIN WEASEL MUST HAVE SEARCH PARTIES OUT LOOKING FOR US.
YEAH. THESE PASSAGES WILL SOON BE SWARMING WITH FOXES!
WE NEED TO SOLVE THE RIDDLE OF RAB-E-BUNS' SCROLL AS SOON AS POSSIBLE!
?
!
?

# Episode Ten

# THE FINAL RIDDLE OF RAB-E-BUNS

THAT'S IT!
THE CEILING!
IT'S PAINTED WITH HARES...
"FOLLOW THE TUNNEL BENEATH THE HARES ON OUR HEAD..."
BRILLIANT! ...SO THE TUNNEL WILL BE BENEATH THIS PART OF THE CEILING...
YEAH, LOOK HERE...
ANOTHER HARE...
IF I PRESS HIS TAIL...
PAWS CROSSED.
THE SECRET BURROW!

WHAT AN INCREDIBLE PLACE!
AND LOOK! THERE'S THE ETERNAL FLAME LIT BY RAB·E·BUNS ALL THOSE THOUSANDS OF YEARS AGO. AND IT'S STILL ALIGHT!
THIS PLACE IS EVEN MORE AMAZING THAN I IMAGINED!
TUTENKHABAGE WAS ONE WEALTHY RABBIT.
HEY, NO TIME FOR CHATTER... WHAT ABOUT THE LAST VERSE OF THAT RIDDLE?
HOW DID IT GO AGAIN? ..."PRESS THE I IN THE MONSTER THAT'S DEAD."

MM. SEE ANY MONSTERS?
NO, THANK GOODNESS.
ME NEITHER.
HEY, THIS LOOKS INTERESTING...
A CROCODILE MADE FROM GOLD!
A CROCODILE, YES, BUT KNOWN TO THE ANCIENT BUNGYPTIANS AS "THE MONSTER OF DEATH."
THE MONSTER THAT'S DEAD!

EXACTLY, AND WITH GNASHERS LIKE THAT IT'S JUST AS WELL!
MM. IT SEEMS TO ME THERE'S SOMETHING STRANGE ABOUT THOSE EYES.
"THEN PRESS THE EYE IN THE MONSTER THAT'S DEAD!"
GREAT FIELDS OF BROCCOLI, THIS COULD BE IT!
THE CARROTS OF DOOM!!!

# Episode Eleven

# AYE, EYE, CAPTAIN

THE CARROTS OF DOOM!
THAT SILVER IS SO BRIGHT!
BRIGHT AND BEAUTIFUL!
OH NO, NOT HIM AGAIN!

BAD LUCK, FLUFFY COTTON TAILS, LOOKS LIKE YOU MISSED OUT ON THE BIG PRIZE THIS TIME!
JUST IMAGINE... I'LL BE ABLE TO TURN EVERY VEGETABLE ON COLONY 27X INTO PURE GOLD!
THE RABBITS WILL STARVE AND I'LL BE A ZILLIONAIRE.*
HA·HA·HA·HA·HA!
I HATE THAT LAUGH OF HIS.
I THOUGHT THE BAD WEASELS WEREN'T SUPPOSED TO WIN!
WHAT HAPPENS NEXT?
STAND ASIDE, YOU SAD LITTLE LETTUCE-EATERS! MAKE WAY FOR THE NEXT RULER OF COLONY 27X!

* er, very rich.

STRANGE, BUT THEY SEEM TO BE STRUCK.
WAIT, THAT'S BETTER, I'VE GOT TO THEM NOW!
JUST A TOUCH MORE...
Suddenly, the jaw of the golden crocodile gave a loud groan and snapped shut.
SNAP!
!
HEY! STOP PLAYING AROUND! OPEN UP!!!
IT LOOKS LIKE THAT CROC WAS BOOBY-TRAPPED!
AND CAPTAIN WEASEL FELL INTO THE TRAP.

Outside the Fur-O's Pyramid, a storm was raging and the skies were streaked with lightning . . .

Rudley, Cabba, and Rachel knew nothing of this: the sounds of the storm were drowned out by Captain Weasel's squeals.

## Episode Twelve

# STATUE OF LIBERTY

WHAT ABOUT THE CAPTAIN?
HE'LL BE TOO HEAVY TO CARRY, TRAPPED INSIDE THAT GOLDEN CROC.
THIS IS THE VOICE OF RAB-E-BUNS...
AYEEE!
THEY'RE RUNNING AWAY!
HEY, WHAT'S GOING ON?
SSSH...LET'S LISTEN TO THE STATUE...

YOU SEE NOW MY RIDDLE WAS A BIT OF A FIDDLE, AND FOR THAT I APOLOGISE...
BUT THE CARROTS OF DOOM ARE TOO DANGEROUS BY HALF AND THE FUR·O IN HIS WISDOM WAS WISE...
HIS ORDERS WERE GIVEN THE CARROTS WERE HIDDEN... THE ONES YOU SAW WERE FAKES YOU DID WELL ON YOUR QUEST SO DON'T BE DEPRESSED THIS WAY IS BEST FOR ALL OUR SAKES...
THIS ROOM WILL SELF·DESTRUCT IN SIXTY SECONDS.
SIXTY SECONDS! WE'D BETTER MAKE TRACKS. FAST!
HEY! WHAT ABOUT ME!?
AND WHAT ABOUT THE CARROTS OF DOOM?
THERE ARE SOME THINGS IN LIFE MORE IMPORTANT THAN CARROTS... EVEN ANCIENT SILVER ONES.

crack
LOOK! THE ROOM'S BEGINNING TO FILL WITH SAND!
LET'S GET OUT OF HERE BEFORE WE'RE BURROWED ALIVE!
sand
NICE BUNNIES. YOU WOULDN'T LEAVE THE OLD CAPTAIN BEHIND, WOULD YOU?
I WISH WE COULD HELP YOU, CAPTAIN WEASEL, BUT THERE'S NO WAY WE CAN LIFT THIS GOLDEN CROCODILE!

RUDLEY! COME ON, BEFORE IT'S TOO LATE!
JUST ONE LAST LOOK... THIS IS THE LAST TIME ANY RABBIT WILL SEE THESE TREASURES.
AND I WONDER IF THE REAL CARROTS OF DOOM ARE HIDDEN HERE, SOMEWHERE?
RUDLEY, OVER HERE, THE TUNNEL IS ALMOST BLOCKED!
The eternal flame gave one last flicker and Rab-E-Buns' secret chamber plunged into darkness . . .
I'D FORGOTTEN HOW FAST THESE RABBITS HOP WHEN THEY'RE IN TROUBLE!
I'D FORGOTTEN HOW SLOW THESE HUMANS ARE!
small carving taken for archaeological study

# Episode Thirteen

# DAWN OVER BUNZA

RAVISHING RADISHES, OF COURSE! SO CAPTAIN WEASEL WAS CLOSER THAN HE KNEW!
AND IT WAS ONLY RAB·E·BUNS' LAST TRICK WHICH SAVED THE DAY!
FORTUNATELY THE CARROTS ARE BURIED NOW FOR ALL TIME.
ALONG WITH CAPTAIN WEASEL...
...AND MY BEST TORCH!
DON'T WORRY ABOUT THAT...
THE MAIN THING IS THAT WE OUT·FOXED THOSE FOXES, AND THAT CAPTAIN WEASEL WON'T TROUBLE US EVER AGAIN...
SO WHY DO I HAVE THE FEELING WE HAVEN'T SEEN THE LAST OF HIM?!
The End